Passport to Genre

A Literature Enrichment Guide

WRITTEN BY **DEBBIE CONNOLLY** & **LAURIE DANLEY**

ILLUSTRATED BY **CORBIN HILLAM**

Teaching & Learning Company
1204 Buchanan St., P.O. Box 10
Carthage, IL 62321-0010

This book belongs to

_____

Cover art by Corbin Hillam

Copyright © 2006, Teaching & Learning Company

ISBN-13: 978-1-57310-488-3
ISBN-10: 1-57310-488-4

Printing No. 987654321

Teaching & Learning Company
1204 Buchanan St., P.O. Box 10
Carthage, IL 62321-0010

Table of Contents

Dear Teacher or Parent,

The genre passport began simply as a way to motivate the students in our classes to read and experience different genres rather than getting "stuck" in certain genres and series.

We began with a common genre wheel and an assortment of stickers. The incentive for students was to finish two genre wheels and earn 100 points in a self-selected reading program for a reward of a "sleepover" in the school library at the end of the year. To finish a wheel, they had to read a book in their reading zone and score 80% or better on a comprehension test, earning a sticker in that genre on their wheel. That first year, our students became voracious genre readers.

The second year we set monthly goals for each student and tied this into the incentive sleepover. Again, the year was a great success. Our library staff had so many requests for books from different genres they wondered what we had been up to. We gave them a wheel and explained what we were doing to help them guide students towards books in their reading zones and find books in certain genres.

The next year the genre contracts were developed, to be completed by individual students or used with genre book clubs.

When our principal presented us with the Pioneer Award for our work in exploring genres, he asked the student body to raise their hands if they knew what a genre wheel was. Three hundred students enthusiastically waved their hands. He asked them to tell some of their favorite genres, and they began shouting out their favorites. It was rewarding to see the enthusiasm generated by our genre study.

The wheel evolved into its current form, the genre passport, because we wanted more student ownership, more cohesion and a stronger organization. Students still work on their contracts, but have passports instead of wheels. Successful completion of all requirements gets a stamp in their passports.

The genre passport is highly motivating to students. Most have discovered books and genres they may never have read otherwise, and it's an opportunity for meaningful "book talks" or conversations about the wonderful books they have read.

Sincerely,

Debbie Laurie

Debbie Connolly & Laurie Danley

How Genre Passports Work

HOW ARE PASSPORTS ASSEMBLED AND STORED?

Included in this book is the fold-up passport book, pages 12-13. Make copies of it and assemble the passports. Instructions are provided on page 11. When this is completed, display your class' passports in pocket charts, or anything that makes them easily accessible to students.

HOW DO STUDENTS IDENTIFY A GENRE?

The posters, pages 39-53, define the elements of 12 different genres.* A brief summary is also found in the passport itself. Students use these descriptions to complete an activity in the contract titled "The Genre Is . . ." which has them critically examine the elements of genre and provide proof that the book is of the genre they claim.

HOW ARE STAMPS ON THE PASSPORTS EARNED?

The teacher needs to set criteria for students to earn a stamp for a specific genre. This will work with a basal series, since most short stories in anthologies contain different genres. The student chooses a book and meets with the teacher to decide which activities in a contract to be responsible for. There are three types of contracts: fiction, nonfiction and biography, each containing activities for exploring the literary elements specific to each genre. After the student reads the selection, he takes a comprehension test or task. A score of 80% or better is the expected outcome. Meeting all of the above requirements, earns a stamp in the passport for the genre completed. Students can stamp their own passports as they finish or at a designated time.

HOW DO GENRE PASSPORTS FIT INTO YOUR LANGUAGE ARTS PROGRAM?

Besides having a required reading series with an anthology, we use a leveled, self-selected reading program for individual reading practice and run book clubs or literature circles. The genre passport can be easily adapted for use with any type of literature approach.

BASAL READER

Most anthologies include different genres. As you use the anthology's selections, determine the genre and teach the selection within your regular reading instruction. Add the genre contract for students to complete individually, in pairs or in small groups, depending on the student's abilities. Students take the comprehension quiz that comes with the series, complete the contract and if all the requirements are met, earn a stamp in that genre. It doesn't add much work for the teacher and is more motivating for students.

*Copy these and post them in the classroom.

Book Clubs/Literature Circles

A few times a year we used complete literary pieces in our reading instruction. The genre passports fit easily into this context. Students were grouped by level or book choice, depending on how we formed our clubs. The contracts were assigned and books read using the literature circle model. At the end, comprehension tests or activities were completed as were the contracts. When students met the requirements, they earned stamps in their passports.

Independent Reading/Self-Selected Reading

The genre passports fit perfectly with independent reading practice, especially those which have tests. If you do not have such a program, other criteria must be set to evaluate students' comprehension. A written summary can work here, since the teacher cannot possibly read all the books the students read. Using the passport with individual reading practice, students choose a book and determine the genre. Then they meet with the teacher and set up their contract (choosing items they will be responsible for completing). Then they read the selection, take the comprehension test or complete a task and finish the contract, earning a stamp in the passport.

Summary

- Choose a book or short story selection in a certain genre.
- Set up a genre contract with the teacher.
- Read the selection.
- Complete a comprehension task (test, summary, etc.).
- Complete the genre contract.

What Is a Passport?

Most children in your classroom probably have no knowledge of what a passport is or how it is used. It is important therefore, to give them some background that will make the passport relevant and exciting to use.

Encourage them to think of a passport as a special hall pass, an official document or item that authorizes the holder to leave the classroom, move freely through the school, enter another room or space within the building, then return to the classroom again. Trying to do this without a hall pass is risky.

In the same way, a passport is an official document that authorizes the holder to move about outside the country of origin. With a passport a person can visit other countries and experience other cultures, then return home again. Trying to do this without a passport is risky. When entering and leaving each country, a traveler must show the passport so it can be stamped with an official stamp of that country.

If you have a passport, bring it to class and show it to your students. Let them examine it closely.

Materials Management

There are as many ways to manage genre passport materials as there are teachers. One of the advantages of *Passport to Genre* is that it is easily adaptable to any teaching/learning environment. Keep in mind that it needs to be easily accessible to teacher and students. Think about the age, ability level and degree of homogeneity of your students. Do you need more organization, more teacher control, more specific activities; or would your situation call for more student-directed activities, less organization and more spontaneity? *Passport to Genre* lets you choose the most appropriate approach for your situation. Some examples of ways we have organized the genre passports are:

- Copy all contracts and support materials and place them in labeled folders in a file cabinet or file box. Make sure students know they are not to take the last copy. When only two copies remain, they turn one in the vertical position to signal that the file needs to be replenished.

- Label and store contracts and support materials in desktop stacking trays on a countertop. When one gets low, students signal the need for more as explained above.

Organizing materials so they are easily accessible will save a lot of time and put the responsibility on your students. Help students find ways to organize their materials. A two-pocket folder works very well. Students know that everything related to their genre passports is kept in the genre folder.

THE PROCESS FOR THE STUDENT

1. Choose a book (or the next short story from anthology, or book club book).
2. Identify the genre using posters and passport.
3. Have a meeting with the teacher to set goals on the contract and sign.
4. Gather support materials needed to complete the contract. Keep them in the genre folder.
5. Read the selection.
6. Complete the test or comprehension activity.
7. Complete the contract activities. Staple all finished work to the back of the contract and hand it in.
8. If all requirements are successfully met, as determined by the contract, stamp the passport.
9. Choose a new genre.
10. Repeat the process.

Record Keeping

STAMPS

The teacher maintains control of the stamp. How and when a passport is stamped is up to the teacher.

Suggestions

1. One or two days a week, students who have successfully completed a genre contract meet with the teacher to have their passports stamped. (We usually did this during independent reading time.)
2. Students earn their stamps as they finish each contract.

Fit this into your busy schedule where it makes the most sense and when you have the time. The important thing is to let students stamp their own passports. They take great pride in this.

SETTING GOALS

Set goals with individual students or with a small group, depending on the instructional setting. Once a genre is decided upon, the student meets with the teacher and they decide together what the requirements will be for that contract. (Contracts are located in the resource section of this book on pages 14-16.) The following literary elements for the fiction contract are determined at this meeting:

1. Proof of Genre
The Genre Is . . . This is required for all contracts. The student needs to come up with three examples from the story to support the genre type.

2. Character
There are four activities from which to choose:

- *Describing the Main Character Web*
- *Character Development Story Map*
- *Character Trait Map*
- *Compare & Contrast Characters*

3. Setting
There are two activities from which to choose:

- *Literary Elements of Setting*
- *The 5 Ws of Story*

Choose one activity and check it off.

4. Plot
There are five activities from which to choose:

- *Sequencing Events of Story/Plot*
- *Plot Graphic Organizer*
- *Cause & Effect*
- *Elements of Plot*
- *Plot Diamond*

Choose one activity and check it off.

5. Literary Critiques
There are two activities from which to choose:

- *Literary Reactions*
- *Opinion & Support*

Choose one activity and check it off.

6. End-of-Book Projects

In the resource section you will find a list of end-of-book projects, pages 36-38. This is by no means a complete list. You probably have projects you have successfully used in the past. You may wish to control the project selection by limiting the choices to five or so, or you may be comfortable presenting the entire list.

When the requirements of the contract have been decided, the student and teacher both sign the contract. The student then gathers the needed materials for the contract and begins to read the book.

The Nonfiction and Biography contracts offer different choices appropriate to the genre. The same goal setting process is followed with all contracts. You will find them in the resource section, pages 14-15.

TLC10488 Copyright © Teaching & Learning Company, Carthage, IL 62321-0010

Assembling the Passport

1. Copy pages 12 and 13 onto 11" x 17" paper.
2. Trim away border to passport outline.
3. Fold in half lengthwise to 5½" x 17", picture side out.
4. Unfold. Fold in half the opposite way for a 9" x 11" piece, picture side out.
5. Fold in half once more in the same direction as the last fold in step #3 so the cover page and the Adventure and Animal Fiction page are on the front.
6. Unfold the last fold made to have a 9" x 11" piece again.
7. Cut **from the folded edge** along the <u>bold</u> line to the center of the page.
8. Unfold to 11" x 17". Refold lengthwise once more as in step #2.
9. Pick up the 5½" x 17" strip by the ends. When you push the ends toward each other, the center, where the cut was made, should separate, forming a diamond opening in center. Continue to push your hands toward each other until it collapses, or closes.
10. Carefully fold all the pages together to create the book.

Assembling the Travel Brochure (pages 60-61)

1. Copy page 60, then copy page 61 on the back of page 60.

2. Fold the brochure in thirds so *The State of Imagination* is on the front.

3. Give every student a copy of the brochure and encourage them to read it, then share it with a friend.

Mystery

* Plot involves uncovering and piecing together clues
* A definite single problem is set, worked out and solved

Humor

* Events may be farfetched or exaggerated
* Causes the reader to laugh

Historical Fiction

* Story based on an earlier era or time period
* May be a fictionalized account of a real person or event

Folktale/Legend/Myth

* Passed down from generation to generation
* Teaches moral lessons
* Explains natural phenomena otherwise difficult to explain
* Characters have

Newbery/Caldecott

* Prestigious award in children's literature or illustration

Realistic Fictions

* Story is believable—could have actually happened

Nonfiction

* Factual
* Research based

Science Fiction/Spooky

* Story with plot based on scientific theory
* Sense of dark, unknown forces
* Frightful
* Haunted houses, monsters, etc.

Copy pages 12 and 13 onto 11" x 17" paper and fold according to directions on page 11.

Passport to Genre

_____'s

Adventure

* Thriller
* Race against time
* Full of chases, showdowns, rescues
* Heart-racing plot

Biography

* A life history of an individual, living or not

Animal Fiction

* Animal as a main character
* Action revolves around what animal does/needs
* Animal acts as real animal
* Animal has a realistic problem

Fantasy/Fairy Tale

* Not real/disbelief is the key
* Characters may have special powers: magic, ability to travel where others can't, etc.

Fiction Contract

NAME _____ DATE _____

BOOK TITLE _____

AUTHOR _____

GENRE _____

1. PROOF OF GENRE

_____ The Genre Is . . .

2. CHARACTER (Choose ~~one.~~ *two*)

_____ Describing the Main Character Web

_____ Character Development Story Map

_____ Character Trait Map

_____ Compare & Contrast Characters

3. SETTING (~~Choose one.~~ *Do both*)

_____ Literary Elements of Setting

_____ The 5 Ws of Story

4. PLOT (Choose ~~one.~~ *3*)

_____ Sequencing Events of Story/Plot

_____ Plot Graphic Organizer

_____ Cause & Effect

_____ Elements of Plot

_____ Plot Diamond

5. LITERARY CRITIQUES (Choose one.)

_____ Literary Reactions

_____ Opinion & Support

6. END-OF-BOOK PROJECT (Choose one from list.)

STUDENT SIGNATURE _____

TEACHER SIGNATURE _____

COMPREHENSION ACTIVITY SCORE _____

CONTRACT COMPLETED _____

Nonfiction Contract

NAME _____ DATE _____

BOOK TITLE _____

AUTHOR _____

GENRE _____

1. ____ The Genre Is . . .

2. ____ SQ3R
____ KWL
____ Book Report—Nonfiction

3. END-OF-BOOK PROJECT

Choose one option from list.

STUDENT SIGNATURE _____

TEACHER SIGNATURE _____

COMPREHENSION ACTIVITY SCORE _____

CONTRACT COMPLETED _____

Biography Contract

NAME _____ DATE _____

BOOK TITLE _____

AUTHOR _____

GENRE _____

1. PROOF OF GENRE

____ The Genre Is . . .

2. CHARACTER

____ Describing the Main Character Web

____ V.I.P. Form

3. TIME LINE

Cut and paste as many frames as needed.

4. END-OF-BOOK PROJECT

Choose one appropriate option from list.

STUDENT SIGNATURE _____

TEACHER SIGNATURE _____

COMPREHENSION ACTIVITY SCORE _____

CONTRACT COMPLETED _____

The Genre Is . . .

_____

BOOK TITLE: _____

Thoroughly describe three examples from your book that prove that it is of this genre.

ADDITIONAL DETAILS

Describing the Main Character Web

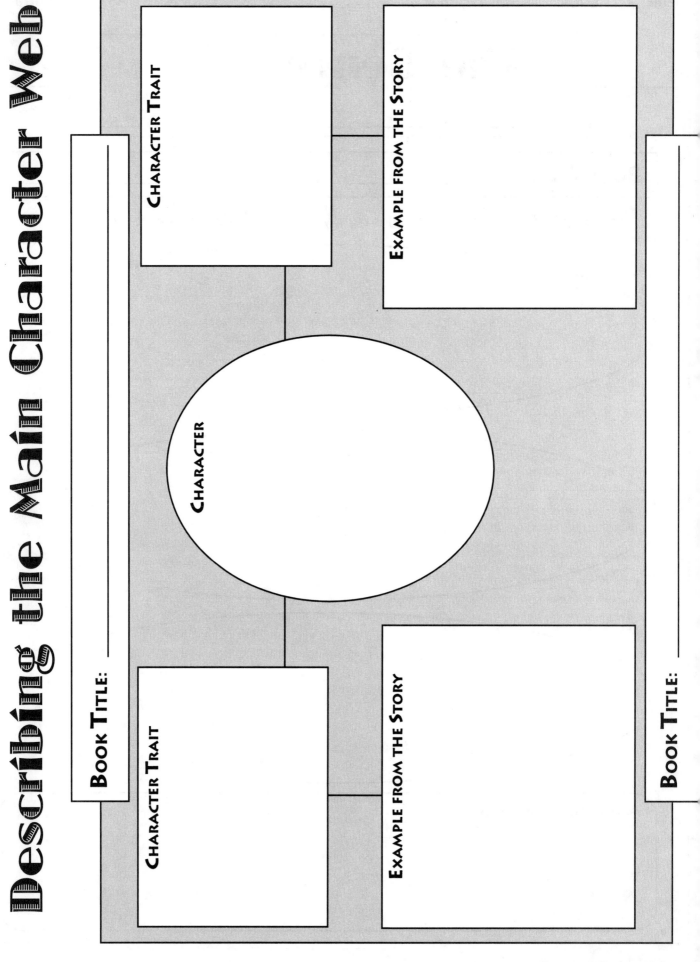

BOOK TITLE: _____

CHARACTER TRAIT

EXAMPLE FROM THE STORY

CHARACTER

CHARACTER TRAIT

EXAMPLE FROM THE STORY

BOOK TITLE: _____

Character Development Story Map

BOOK TITLE: _____

CHARACTER: _____

IN THE BEGINNING . . .

How does the character act?

How does the character feel?

How does the character act?

How does the character feel?

What happened in the story that caused this change?

LATER . . .

Write the character's name and the title of the book in the top box. Put one character trait in each star. Give two supporting details from the story for each trait given in the boxes at the bottom.

CHARACTER'S NAME & BOOK TITLE

TRAIT

TRAIT

DETAIL

DETAIL

DETAIL

DETAIL

Character Trait Map

Name _____

Compare & Contrast Characters

CHARACTER'S NAME

CHARACTER'S NAME

Differences

Similarities

Differences

21

Literary Elements of Setting

BOOK TITLE: _____

Seeing

Smelling/Tasting

Where: _____

When: _____

Feeling

Hearing

The 5 Ws of Story

Fill in each box with detailed answers to the questions.

WHAT HAPPENED?

WHO WAS THERE?

WHERE DID IT HAPPEN?

WHEN DID IT HAPPEN?

WHY DID IT HAPPEN?

Sequencing Events of Story/Plot

BOOK TITLE: _____

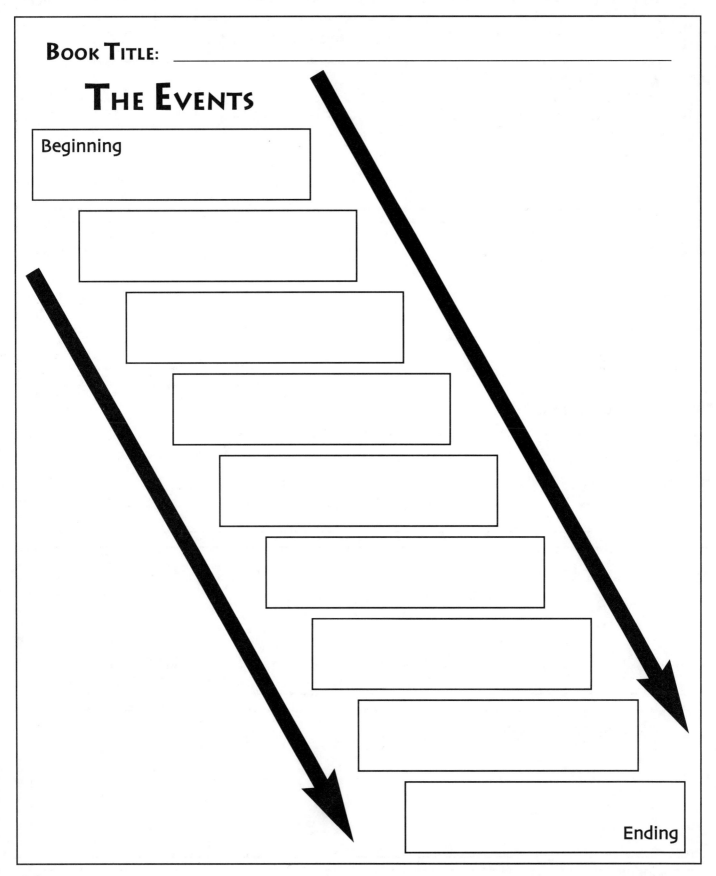

THE EVENTS

Beginning

Ending

Plot Graphic Organizer

BOOK TITLE: _____

Who are the main characters and where does the story take place?

What did the characters want to do? What did they hope to achieve?

Was there a problem?
Did something really exciting happen?

How was the problem solved?

How did the solution impact other characters in the story?

Cause & Effect

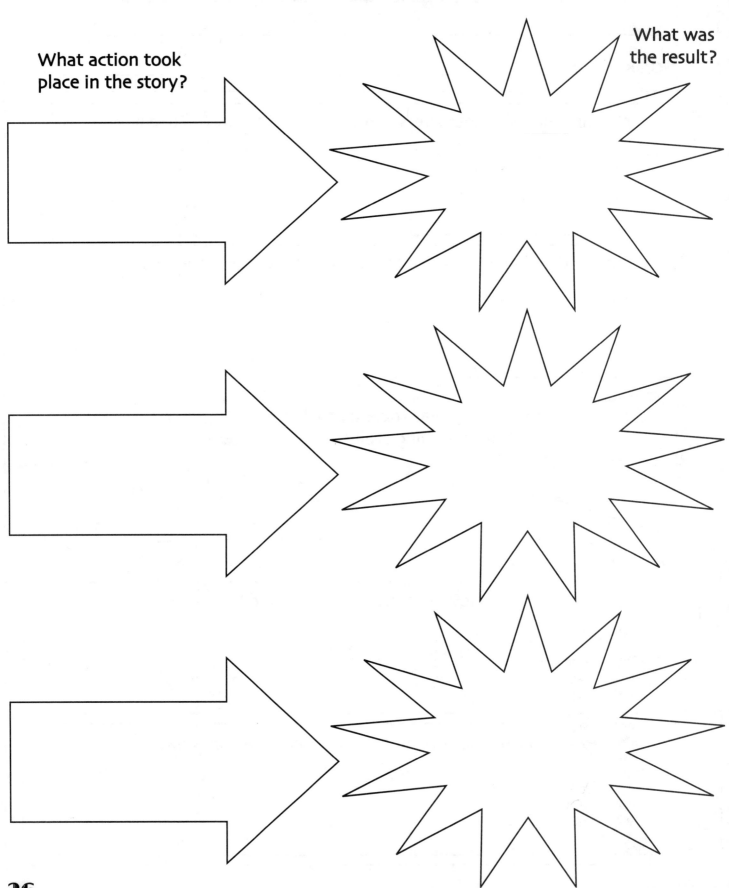

What action took place in the story?

What was the result?

BOOK TITLE

Elements of Plot

Describe the climax of the story.
(when the action reaches its highest point)

How does the main character(s) solve the problem?

How else could the problem have been solved?

Name the main characters who are involved in the conflict.

What choices do/does the main character(s) have?

Describe the conflict (problem) the main character(s) is/are facing.

Name _____

Plot Diamond

Book Title: _____

1. Name of the main character.
2. Two words that describe the main character.
3. Three words that describe the setting.
4. Four words stating the problem in the story.
5. Five words that describe one event in the story.
6. Four words that describe a second event.
7. Three words that describe a third event.
8. Two words that describe the solution to the problem.
9. One word that describes a change in the character.

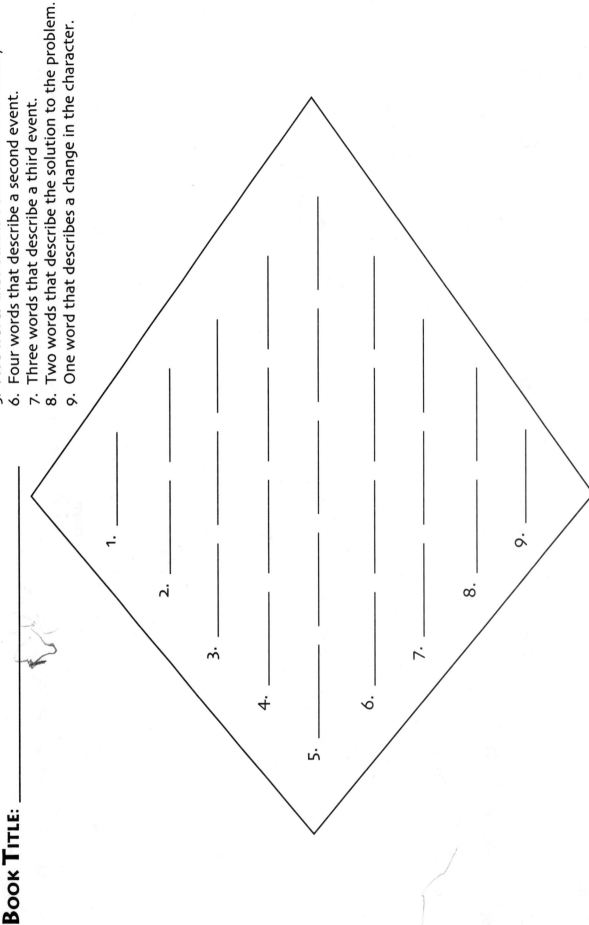

Name _____

Literary Reactions

BOOK TITLE: _____

EVENT Describe what happened.	PERSONAL REACTION How do you feel about it?

Name _____

Opinion & Support

BOOK TITLE: _____

OPINION

SUPPORTING DETAIL

SUPPORTING DETAIL

SUPPORTING DETAIL

SQ3R: Survey, Question, Read, Recite, Review

SURVEY: Before reading skim over the selection. Resist reading at this time. Try to determine three or more major topics or ideas in the selection and list them below.

```


```

QUESTION: Ask yourself these questions: What is this text about? What would I like to learn?

```


```

READ: Read slowly and carefully while trying to find the answers to your questions. Find a place free of distractions. Concentrate.

RECITE/WRITE: Below write the answers to your questions *in your own words*. You will remember the information *much* longer if you do.

```


```

REVIEW: Write a short paragraph in your own words summarizing the selection.

```


```

KWL

Book Title: _____

What Do I Know?	**What Do I WANT to Know?**	**What Did I LEARN?**
(before reading)	(before reading)	(after reading)

Book Report—Nonfiction

TITLE: _____

AUTHOR: _____

What was this book about?

[ ]

What are some things you learned by reading?

[ ]

Would you recommend this book to someone else?

[ ]

Why do you think the author wrote this book?

[ ]

V.I.P.: Very Important Person

This Very Important Person is: _____

Date of Birth: _____ Date of Death: _____

He or she came from: _____

Why this book was written about this V.I.P.

[ ]

Why he or she did these things (made to . . .   chose to . . .)

[ ]

Things to admire about this person

[ ]

Things *not* to admire about this person

[ ]

Name _____

TIME LINE OF _____

DATE _____

DATE _____

DATE _____

DATE _____

End-of-Book Projects

Following are a number of projects. When appropriate, specific genres are identified that work well with a project. Otherwise the projects are generic.

1. Biographies/Autobiographies: Create a life-sized model or poster of your favorite character and dress him or her as dressed in the book. Include 10 facts about the character that describe and tell of his or her role in the book. Present it to the class.

2. Interview a character from your book. Write 10 questions to give the character a chance to talk about himself or herself and thoughts and feelings about the role he or she played in the story. Present the interview in a written news story or oral report.

3. Write a diary from the point of view of your character. Include the character's thoughts and feelings along with the events as they happened.

4. Dramatize a scene from your book. Write a script, rehearse and present it to your class. (This works great with literature circles when a group of students are reading the same book. Good small group project.)

5. One-Minute Oral Book Report. (This is timed and a practiced speaking presentation.) In one minute, give the important particulars (characters, setting, plot) of the book. Be prepared for questions from the class.

6. Draw sketches of some of your favorite scenes from the book. Label them and write a brief description about the events that occurred.

7. Write a book review for a newspaper or magazine. Be sure to read some reviews before writing your own.

8. Construct a diorama, a three-dimensional scene, from your book. Include a written description of the scene.

9. Write a feature article, including a headline, from a newspaper in the town where the story takes place that tells the story of your book.

10. Write a letter to the main character of your book. Ask questions, make comments or make a complaint or suggestion. Use correct letter form.

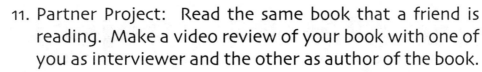

11. Partner Project: Read the same book that a friend is reading. Make a video review of your book with one of you as interviewer and the other as author of the book.

12. Prepare a travel brochure about the place where your book happens. Use in your brochure pictures you have found or drawn.

13. Draw a portrait of your main character(s). Write a complete description of the character, physical, emotional and social.

14. Historical Fiction or History Nonfiction: Create an illustrated time line showing events from the story.

15. Nonfiction: Read two books on the same subject, then compare and contrast them using a Venn diagram.

16. If your book has been made into a movie, write an essay comparing the two.

17. Make a comic strip mini book of a chapter in your book.

18. Create a poster about your book. Include all the important information.

19. Be a television or radio reporter. Give a "live" report from a scene in your book as if you are there as it is happening.

20. Design a book jacket for your book. Check out some book jacket covers to make sure you include everything.

21. Give a book talk to the class. Tell about the author, characters and beginning of the story. Then read an exciting or interesting part of the story aloud. Stop reading at an interesting point and say, "If you want to know more, you'll have to read . . ." Watch *Reading Rainbow* book reviews on television to get the idea.

22. Make a mobile about your story. Include the title and a brief description of author, characters and setting.

23. Write a different beginning or ending for your story.

24. Write a letter to the author of your book. Describe what you liked and didn't like or ask the author questions. Write in correct letter form. Mail it to the author if possible.

25. Make a map of where events in the book took place. Label each and write a brief description of the event.

26. Create a poster advertising your book to make other students want to read it.

27. Learn something about the environment in which your book takes place. Research and write an essay about the environment.

28. Nonfiction: Write 10 things you learned while reading.

29. Fantasy/Folktales/Fables: Write part of the story in your own words from a different character's point of view.

30. Choose the climax of your story. Change one thing that happened; write how it would have affected the outcome.

31. Write a one-sentence summary of each chapter of your book and illustrate the sentence to make a mini book.

32. Make a bookmark for the book. Draw a character in the setting and list the book's title, author, genre and a brief summary.

33. Write a multiple choice quiz about your book with at least 10 questions. If someone else has read your book, have that person take your quiz.

34. Pretend you could spend a day with one of the characters from your book. Write about the day and why you chose that character.

35. Write a plot for the sequel to your book. Include new characters, the setting and what the problem is.

36. Rewrite and illustrate your story in picture book format for younger kids.

37. Make game boards using the Chutes and Ladders format. Use events from the story as ways for students to move forward or go back. (This can be a group or partner project.)

38. Put together a Power Point presentation about your book, using images and music to tell about it.

39. Create a project of your own ideas!

Humor

Events may be farfetched or exaggerated

Causes the reader to laugh

Nonfiction

Factual

Research based

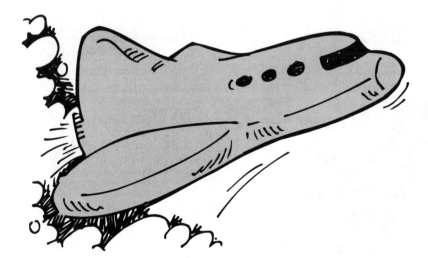

Newbery/ Caldecott

Prestigious award in children's literature or illustration

Look for the gold or silver seal on the book cover.

Adventure

Thriller

Race against time

Full of chases, showdowns, rescues

Heart-racing plot

Animal Fiction

Animal as a main character

Action revolves around what animal does/needs

Animal acts as real animal

Main human character tied to animal character

Animal has a realistic problem

Biography

A life history of an individual, living or not

Fantasy

Not real/disbelief is the key

Characters may have special powers: magic, ability to travel where others can't, etc.

Folktale

Explains natural phenomena otherwise difficult to explain

Describes adventure of an epic character

Teaches moral lesson and respectable values

Passes down customs, beliefs and traditions

Legend

Characters have special traits

Based on a fictional or real figure whose story has been exaggerated

Passed from one generation to the next

Reveals a lesson to the reader

Myth

Includes god, goddess, hero, etc.

Contains magic or characters with special powers

Provides an explanation for unknown events,
natural phenomena or human behavior

Moral lesson about humanity;
may not have a happy ending

Historical Fiction

Story is based on an earlier era or time period

Characters are entirely fictional or
based on a real person in history

Mystery

Plot involves uncovering
and piecing together clues

A definite single problem is set,
worked out and solved

Realistic Fiction

Everything in the story could happen to real people

Does not have to be true but
could have happened

Spooky

Frightful

Sense of dark, unknown forces

Haunted houses, monsters, etc.

Science Fiction

Story with plot based on scientific theory

Believable plots

HUMOR

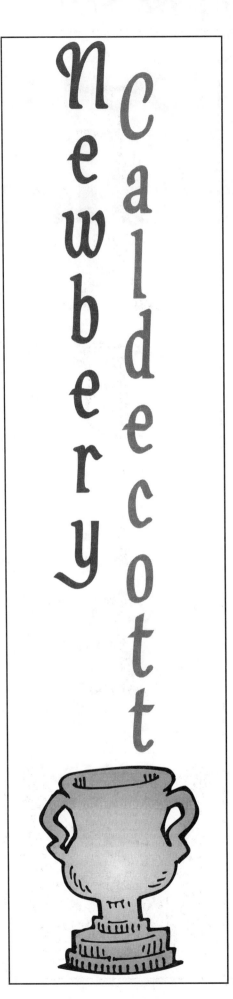

Newbery Caldecott

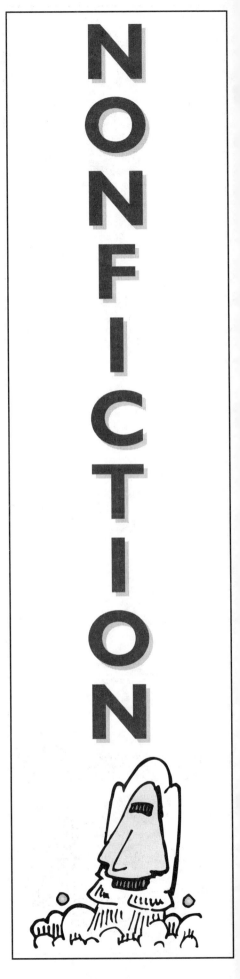

NONFICTION

54

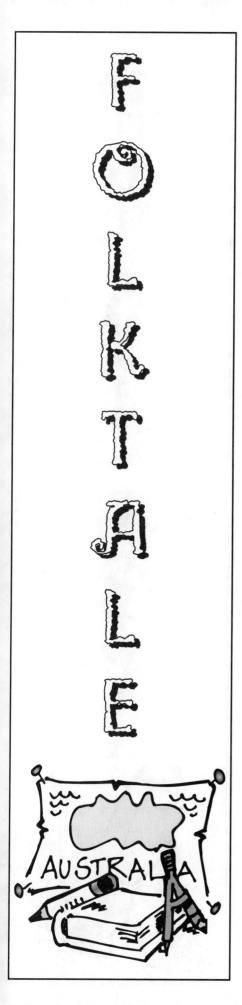

FOLKTALE

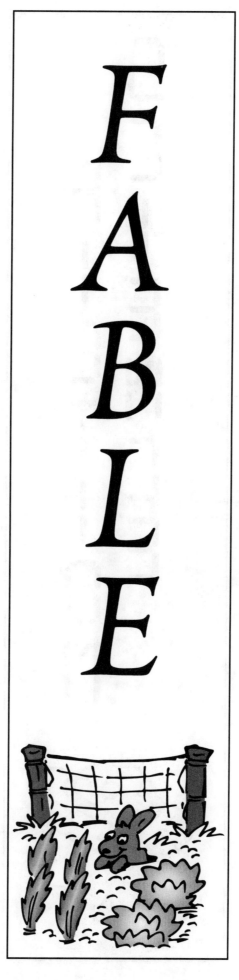

FABLE

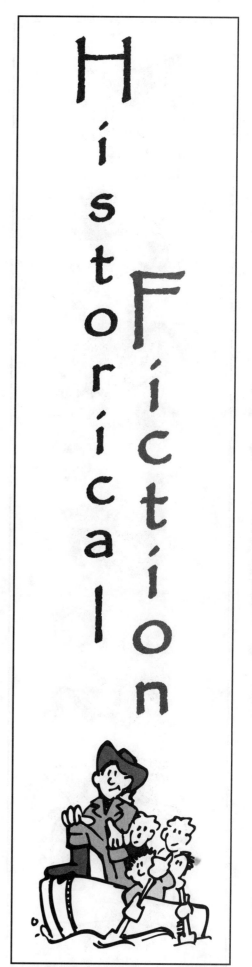

Historical Fiction

Animal Fiction

Science Fiction

Mystery

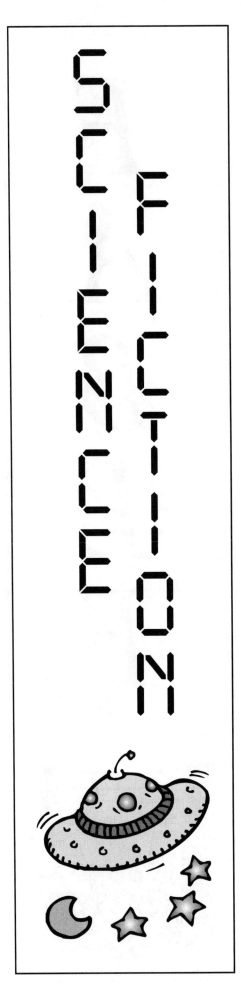

Fantasy

ADVENTURE

BIOGRAPHY

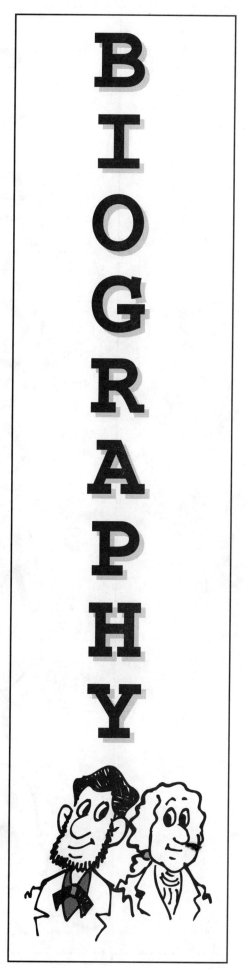

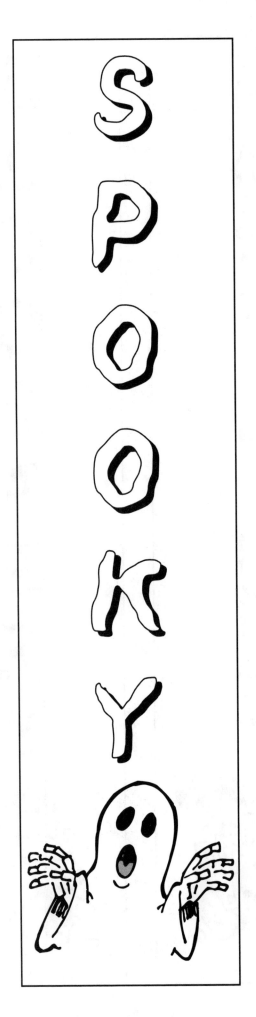

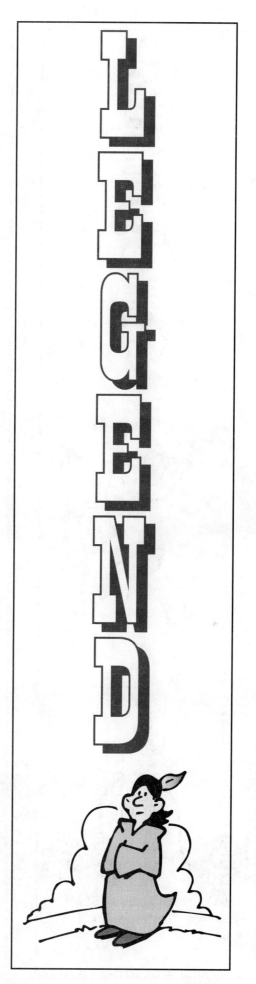

The State of Imagination

There is no limit to the wonderful places you'll go and amazing things you'll see.

Lose yourself in a good book! Do it today!

ADVENTURE
BIOGRAPHY
FOLKTALE
HUMOR
MYSTERY
NONFICTION
SCIENCE FICTION
ANIMAL FICTION
FANTASY/FAIRY TALE
LEGEND/MYTH
HISTORICAL FICTION
NEWBERY/CALDECOTT
REALISTIC FICTION
SPOOKY

Take the leap! Let a good book and your imagination take you to new and exciting experiences.

Visit your school library.

Take a trip to the public library.

Ask your teacher, your librarian and your friends for their favorite book recommendations.

Then sit back, read and explore.

60

Where Would You Like to Go?

Reading is the only way to travel through the State of Imagination. A good book is the avenue by which you can travel to any number of wonderful and interesting experiences. The book you choose will be your ticket into a unique genre. Here are a few of the possibilities.

The Past They Say Is History

Would you like to take an epic journey with a wagon train that will last five months, walking hundreds and hundreds of miles on foot? Perhaps a nice long sail on a three-masted schooner, sailing the high seas and searching for new worlds or fantastic treasures is more to your liking. Perhaps you would enjoy racing a chariot through ancient Rome. When you dig into the genre **historical fiction**, there is no limit to the adventures you'll have. If it's happened and been written about, you can live it, too! Take a trip into a **historical fiction** novel.

Do You Crave Suspense?

If it is an edge-of-your-seat experience you crave, visit the genre **spooky**. This is the place where you'll find white-knuckle, heart-pumping, breath-stopping thrills. But don't worry; you don't have to read a book that will cause you to lose sleep and lie trembling in fear. You can visit books that make you hold your breath in suspense without terrifying you. You might find yourself aching to shout out loud or wanting to jump right into the book to help out some hapless victim. Give the genre **spooky** a try.

How About a Little Magic with Your Milk and Cookies?

What would it be like to fight dragons? Better still, wouldn't you love to ride on the back of one as it soars high in the sky? What would you do if you owned your own magic wand? Would you turn everything to chocolate? If the world of unbelievable wonders is your desire, take a trip to the genre of **fantasy**. Tame a wild unicorn. Rub elbows with a robe-clad wizard. Talk to animals. There is no limit to the amazement you will experience in the world of **fantasy**.

What Did You Say?

Would you like to listen in on conversations among a barnyard full of animals? What would they say to each other? "That darn farmer keeps stealing my eggs!" What if animals lived just like humans in medieval times? Would they wield swords and shields and fight fierce battles to protect their castles? When you are in the genre **animal fiction**, amazing things are commonplace. Visit **animal fiction** and experience it for yourself.

Your Ticket to the State of Imagination

You Are Going Places Now!

FANTASY LAND

Fight fierce, fire-breathing dragons! Participate in a medieval jousting competition! Find out what it's like to wear a suit of armor or the royal gown of a medieval princess. These experiences can be yours when you take a trip into a **fantasy** book.

FAR DISTANT GALAXIES

Zip through space in a flying saucer, streaking toward distant stars and planets! Have exciting adventures with strange creatures. Try out some new and unusual foods. The sky's the limit when you immerse yourself in a **science fiction** book.

ANIMAL ADVENTURES

What would it be like to live like your favorite animal, while still being able to think and act like you? Have you ever wished you could experience the life of a dog or cat, a frog or a rat? If so, burrow yourself into an **animal fiction** book.

THE POSSIBILITIES ARE ENDLESS . . .

When you choose a book from your local or school library, you are checking out a passport to another world. The opportunities to explore life beyond your own experiences are just a book jacket away.

Name _____

Reading Log

Date	Book Title	Author	Genre

www Annotated Book Lists by Genre

HISTORICAL FICTION
http://childrensbooks.about.com/gi/dynamic/offsite.htm?zi=1/XJ&sdn=childrensbooks&zu=http%3A%2F%2Fwww.gti.net%2Frocktwp%2Fhistfict.html

A list of intermediate level historical fiction books organized by period.

MYSTERIES FOR INTERMEDIATE KIDS
http://www.ferglib.org/ferg/youth_link/kidol/booklists/mysterybooklist.htm

Briefly annotated mystery book lists for grades one through 6.

HUMOROUS STORIES
http://www.ci.cerritos.ca.us/library/booklists/humorous.html

An extensive, annotated list of popular humor books for children.

ADVENTURE TITLES
http://www.ci.cerritos.ca.us/library/booklists/adventure.html

Another annotated list by City of Cerritos for the Performing Arts, this one of adventure titles for children.

NEWBERY AND CALDECOTT
http://www.ala.org/ala/alsc/awardsscholarships/literaryawds/newberymedal/newberywinners/medalwinners.htm
http://www.ala.org/ala/alsc/awardsscholarships/literaryawds/caldecottmedal/caldecottwinners/caldecottmedal.htm

These are the American Library Association's lists of all Newbery and Caldecott medal winners.

COOL READS
At this site you will find a plethora of book recommendations and reviews by kids ages 10 to 15. The link allows you to sort the list by genre. Some books reviewed here may not be appropriate for your younger readers.

http://www.cool-reads.co.uk/